D1408780

HORSES SET I

PALOMINO HORSES

BreAnn Rumsch
ABDO Publishing Company

visit us at
www.abdopublishing.com

Published by ABDO Publishing Company, 8000 West 78th Street, Edina, Minnesota 55439. Copyright © 2011 by Abdo Consulting Group, Inc. International copyrights reserved in all countries. No part of this book may be reproduced in any form without written permission from the publisher. The Checkerboard Library™ is a trademark and logo of ABDO Publishing Company.

Printed in the United States of America, North Mankato, Minnesota.
042010
092010

 PRINTED ON RECYCLED PAPER

Cover Photo: iStockphoto
Interior Photos: Alamy pp. 5, 16; Animals Animals pp. 7, 11; Getty Images pp. 9, 13; iStockphoto pp. 15, 17, 19; Photolibrary p. 21

Editor: Tamara L. Britton
Art Direction & Cover Design: Neil Klinepier

Library of Congress Cataloging-in-Publication Data

Rumsch, BreAnn, 1981-
  Palomino horses / BreAnn Rumsch.
      p. cm. -- (Horses)
  Includes index.
   ISBN 978-1-61613-420-4
  1. Palomino horse--Juvenile literature. I. Title.
  SF293.P3R86 2011
  636.1'3--dc22

                                                2010009613

CONTENTS

WHERE PALOMINOS CAME FROM

Through the ages, humans have prized horses for their power and beauty. These graceful mammals belong to the family **Equidae**.

A fox-sized creature known as eohippus is the horse's earliest relative. It roamed Earth about 60 million years ago. Over time, horses developed into the many different **breeds** we know today.

The palomino horse has a long history. It has lived since horses were first **domesticated**. Most people believe the palomino descended from the Arabian horse.

Palominos came to North America in the 1500s. Spain's Queen Isabella sent six palominos to Mexico with Spanish explorers. Eventually, these golden horses spread north into present-day Texas and California.

Today, palomino horses are popular for pleasure riding.

What Palominos Look Like

Palominos are not a true horse **breed**. Instead, they are a color type. A color type can occur in many different horse breeds. But, all the horses must share a certain color.

A palomino's weight depends on what breed the horse is. Horse breeds are divided by size into three groups. They are light horses, heavy horses, and ponies.

Most palominos are classified as light horses. Breeds in this group usually weigh less than 1,300 pounds (590 kg). They are the best size for riding.

Usually, palominos stand from 14 to 17 hands high. Each hand equals four inches (10 cm). This measurement is taken from the ground up to the horse's **withers**.

The palomino horse is famous for its special coat color.

What Makes Palominos Special

People have enjoyed palomino horses for thousands of years. They were favorite horses of ancient emperors and kings. They were even represented in Greek myths.

In 1941, palomino lovers formed the Palomino Horse **Breeders** of America (PHBA). This group keeps records of palominos and improves breeding standards.

The palomino color type can occur in every horse breed except the Thoroughbred. However, the PHBA only registers palominos from select breeds. They are quarter horses, American saddlebreds, Arabian horses, Morgans, and Tennessee walking horses.

Quarter horses run fast and turn quickly. Palominos with this breeding are often used for ranching.

COLOR

The palomino is the true golden horse. The ideal coat is the color of a gold coin. The PHBA allows this shade to vary from pale gold to dark gold.

In contrast to its golden coat, the palomino has dark skin. It has black, brown, or hazel eyes. The palomino's mane and tail are white or ivory.

Palomino horses may have white markings on the head and the legs. The most common head markings are a star, a stripe, a **snip**, a **blaze**, and a **bald face**. Common leg markings include ankles, socks, and stockings.

Since palominos are not a **breed**, reproducing their color is tricky. Breeding two palominos only produces palomino horses 50 percent of the time.

Palominos have solid-colored coats. They do not have stripes or spots on the body.

The rest of the time, horses are born either chestnut or cremello. A chestnut horse has a brown coat, mane, and tail. A cremello horse has a cream to light yellow coat. **Breeding** a chestnut with a cremello always produces a palomino.

CARE

Horses depend on their owners for comfortable places to live. In a stable, your palomino needs its own stall with lots of clean bedding. The area should also provide plenty of fresh air.

Keeping your palomino horse healthy is an important part of its care. At least once a year, a veterinarian should examine it. He or she can **deworm** the horse and give it **vaccines**.

The veterinarian can also float your horse's teeth. He or she will check for uneven areas and file them down. This helps the horse chew food properly and avoid mouth problems.

Daily grooming is a great way to keep your palomino healthy. A rubber currycomb and a body brush remove dirt from the horse's coat. A hoof pick keeps dirt and stones out of the horse's hooves.

A horse's hooves need trimming, much like your fingernails do. A farrier should visit your palomino every six to eight weeks. He or she can trim its hooves and replace its horseshoes.

Using the proper grooming tools will help your horse look and feel its best.

FEEDING

A horse's natural food is grass. Wild horses graze on open fields. Stabled horses are fed hay, such as dried grass and alfalfa. They also eat grain, which gives them energy to work. Types of grain include oats, corn, and barley.

A horse should be fed about three times each day. The amount given depends on the horse's size and level of activity.

Horses should always have access to fresh, clean water. Many horses drink 10 to 12 gallons (38 to 45 L) of water each day.

Sometimes, owners also give their horses **supplements**. A salt lick helps a horse replace salt lost while sweating. Cod-liver oil helps improve the horse's coat. Apples and carrots make delicious, healthy treats!

**A manger helps prevent this palomino (left)
from spilling its food.**

THINGS PALOMINOS NEED

Ranchers and trail riders use Western saddles.

Riding a palomino can be exciting! It is most enjoyable when you use the right equipment. Riding equipment is called tack.

The saddle makes the rider more comfortable and protects the horse's back. Saddles are grouped as Western saddles and English saddles. A saddle pad rests under the saddle. It absorbs sweat and prevents the saddle

Many riders use a snaffle bit. It puts pressure on the horse's mouth.

from slipping. Stirrups for the rider's feet attach to the saddle.

The bridle is worn on the horse's head. It includes the bit and the reins. The bit is a metal piece that fits in the horse's mouth. It attaches to the reins, which the rider holds. The rider uses the reins to signal commands to the horse.

All of this tack should fit your horse well to protect it from pain or sores. After riding, always clean your horse's tack. This helps tack last longer. It also protects the horse from dirt and disease. Every horse needs its own tack to prevent spreading germs.

How Palominos Grow

An adult female horse is called a mare. She mates with an adult male called a stallion. Then the mare is **pregnant** for about 11 months. After this time, she gives birth to a baby horse called a foal.

Within one hour after birth, the foal will learn to stand. The foal will drink its mother's milk within the next hour. Soon, the foal's milk teeth begin to grow in. As the young palomino grows, its baby teeth are eventually replaced by permanent teeth.

Palominos develop quickly. After about six months, a foal no longer needs to nurse. At that time, it is **weaned**.

Young palominos spend the next few months with other young horses. Together they play, eat, and learn about being horses. Healthy palominos can live for 20 to 30 years.

Foals form a close bond with their mothers.

TRAINING

Most palominos begin training at a young age. This helps the horses learn to trust people and take directions. One of the first lessons a palomino learns is to wear a halter. This head collar is an important piece of tack. It makes it easier for people to handle the horse.

Preparing a palomino to be ridden requires great skill and patience. A trainer repeats certain words and hand and leg movements. Eventually, the horse understands what these commands mean. Finally, the palomino learns to wear a saddle.

Well-trained palominos can compete in many sports, such as jumping or barrel racing. Cowboys often use them for ranching. No matter its job, a palomino makes a wonderful companion for many years!

Training should be fun for a palomino. This makes the horse willing to learn and eager to please.

GLOSSARY

bald face - a white, wide marking covering most of an animal's face.

blaze - a usually white, broad stripe down the center of an animal's face.

breed - a group of animals sharing the same ancestors and appearance. A breeder is a person who raises animals. Raising animals is often called breeding them.

deworm - to rid of worms.

domesticated - adapted to life with humans.

Equidae (EEK-wuh-dee) - the scientific name for the family of mammals that includes horses, zebras, and donkeys.

pregnant - having one or more babies growing within the body.

snip - a white marking between a horse's nostrils.

supplement - something added to make up for a shortage of substances necessary to health.

vaccine (vak-SEEN) - a shot given to prevent illness or disease.

wean - to accustom an animal to eating food other than its mother's milk.

withers - the highest part of a horse's or other animal's back.

WEB SITES

To learn more about palomino horses, visit ABDO Publishing Company on the World Wide Web at **www.abdopublishing.com**. Web sites about palominos are featured on our Book Links page. These links are routinely monitored and updated to provide the most current information available.

INDEX